RUGBY F CUS
LAWS OF THE GAME

Jon Richards

WAYLAND

First published in 2011 by Wayland

Wayland
338 Euston Road
London NW1 3BH

Wayland Australia
Level 17/207 Kent Street
Sydney, NSW 2000

Editor: Camilla Lloyd
Produced by Tall Tree Ltd
Editor, Tall Tree: Jennifer Sanderson
Designer: Ben Ruocco
Consultant: Tony Buchanan

British Library Cataloguing in Publication Data
  Richards, Jon.
  Rugby focus.
  Laws of the game.
  1. Rugby Union football--Rules--Juvenile literature.
  I. Title
  796.3'3302022-dc22

ISBN: 978 0 7502 6478 5

Printed in China

Wayland is a division of Hachette Children's Books,
an Hachette UK company.

www.hachette.co.uk

Acknowledgements

The author and publisher would like to thank the
following people for their help and participation
in this book: Old Albanian RFC and Neil Dekker.

The website addresses (URLs) included in this book were
valid at the time of going to press. However, because
of the nature of the Internet, it is possible that some
addresses may have changed, or sites may have changed
or closed down since publication. While the author and
Publisher regret any inconvenience this may cause the
readers, no responsibility for any such changes can be
accepted by either the author or the Publisher.

Picture credits

All photography by Michael Wicks, except:
(t – top, l – left, r – right, b – bottom, c – centre)
1, 2, 4, 9bl, 12, 14, 19tr, 23, 28 Santamaradona/
Dreamstime.com; 5 Rixie/Dreamstime.com; 6 Vlana/
Dreamstime.com; 7 Robwilson39/Dreamstime.com;
8, 13, 16, 19br, 26 Dgoodings/Dreamstime.com; 10
tr Jonathanwebley/Dreamstime.com; 19tl Graphitec/
Dreamstime.com; 20, 22, 25l Maccers/Dreamstime.
com; 25r Grosremy/Dreamstime.com; 27r Lukyslukys/
Dreamstime.com; 29 Chris McGrath/Getty Images Sport;
30 Getty Images

CONTENTS

Controlling the game

Rugby is a fast-paced sport, where players regularly make contact with each other. The game has laws controlling what players can and cannot do. These laws deal with how the game is played, while keeping it safe for those playing it.

Fast and furious

The International Rugby Board (IRB) oversees rugby union around the world. It decides which laws to use. There are laws that govern the shape and size of the pitch and how many players are allowed on each team. One of the key features of the sport is that it allows players to run while carrying the ball and to pass the ball by throwing it to team-mates.

BALL IN HAND

The latest edition of the Rugby Union Laws of the Game, published by the IRB, contains 22 separate laws, as well as variations for different versions and age groups.

Aaron Mauger of Leicester looks to pass to his team-mates. Players can pass the ball sideways or backwards – passing the ball forwards will see a scrum awarded to the opposition (see pages 22–23).

Safety first

The health and well-being of the players is the most important consideration in the laws of rugby. Many laws have been changed in order to make the game safer to play. For example, the spear tackle, which sees the tackled player turned upside-down and then slammed head-first into the ground, was outlawed in 2005. Many of the laws regarding safety deal with specific situations, such as the tackle, scrum or maul. However, there are also laws that deal with misconduct. These include serious infringements, such as eye-gouging or kicking. Other safety laws deal with how injured players are treated. These include allowing medical staff to come onto the pitch to treat a serious injury even if the game is still being played, and forcing players who are bleeding to leave the pitch for treatment.

> *Rugby is valued as a sport for men and women, boys and girls. It builds teamwork, understanding, co-operation and respect for fellow athletes.*
>
> IRB Playing Charter 2010

The referee is overseeing a scrum between London Wasps (in black) and Cardiff Blues (in pink). Players must wait for his signal before they engage.

The growing game

The sport is thought to have been started at Rugby School in England. During a football match, a pupil named William Webb Ellis picked up the ball up and ran with it.

Fact or fiction?

Although there is no evidence to confirm how the game of rugby started, Webb Ellis is honoured by having the World Cup trophy named after him. The first laws of the sport were written down at Rugby School in 1845, and during these early years, different schools played under different laws. A group controlling the sport was set up in 1871. It tried to unify the game so that everyone played under the same laws. However, in 1895 a group of clubs from the north of England set up its own code of laws and created the sport of rugby league. The code played by the remaining teams became known as rugby union.

BALL IN HAND

The first sevens tournament was the Melrose Sevens which was held in 1883. The tournament still takes place every year in the same Scottish town.

Rugby sevens is played with just seven players in each team. Several laws have been changed from the full version of the sport for sevens. These include having only three players from each team in a scrum.

Beach rugby is a fast-moving version of the game that is played on a beach pitch. The pitch is much smaller than a full rugby pitch and there are only ten players per team. Five players take part in the match with the other five acting as substitutes. A try is worth one point and no kicks are allowed.

Different versions

Today, the main version of rugby union is played by two teams of 15 players, but there are 'shortened' versions of the game for fewer players. These include rugby tens and rugby sevens.

There are also different laws dealing with different age groups. The youngest players play a version called tag rugby. Here, there is no physical contact allowed and players are tackled by pulling a tag of material that is tucked into the opposition players' shorts. Although tackling is allowed from the age of 11 and upwards, there are still restrictions on what can be done. For example, players cannot be lifted in a lineout until they are 16 years or older.

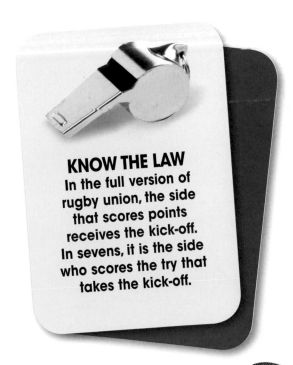

KNOW THE LAW
In the full version of rugby union, the side that scores points receives the kick-off. In sevens, it is the side who scores the try that takes the kick-off.

Referees and assistants

Junior matches and those at lower levels may be overseen by a single referee. High-level games have a team of officials. These include a referee and two assistants or touch judges.

KNOW THE LAW
Before a match, the team captains and the referee will toss a coin. The winner of the coin toss decides whether to kick-off or which end of the pitch to attack.

Men in the middle

Referees have ultimate control over events on the pitch. They decide on whether a law has been broken or whether a player is acting dangerously. Referees indicate their decisions to the players and spectators by using different signals. They also have a number of tasks to perform before the match has kicked off. These include checking to see whether or not the pitch is safe to play on.

The referee is awarding a penalty to English club Northampton. It is the referee's job to ensure the laws are followed and that any infringements are dealt with.

Referee signals

If the ball travels forwards off a hand or arm and hits the ground or another player, the referee will signal a knock-on.

The referee is signalling a scrum. Scrums are used to restart games when minor infringements have occurred.

The referee is indicating a penalty through a high-tackle. Players are not allowed to tackle above shoulder height.

Running the line

The touch judges' main role is to decide whether or not the ball has gone out of play. If it has, they let the referee know by raising a flag. They can also let the referee know if they have seen any foul play that he might have missed. The referee can ask the touch judges for their opinion if a decision is hard to make. The referee can also ask the Television Match Official (TMO) to help with tricky decisions. The TMO can look at video replays and is able to see things from many different angles. Other match-day assistants include time keepers, who keep track of the match time, and touchline assistants, who help when substitutions are made.

A member of a team's coaching staff talks to one of the touchline assistants before a substitution is made.

Players, pitch and ball

Referees check players' equipment and the size of the pitch before a game. They also ensure that the match balls are the correct size and inflated to the correct pressure.

The pitch

Rugby pitches can vary in size, but they must all have certain features that are the same. The entire pitch should not be longer than 100 metres (330 feet) and no wider than 70 metres (230 feet). Running along either side of the pitch are the touchlines, which indicate the edge of the playing area. At either end of the pitch is the tryline and beyond this is the in-goal area. At the back of the in-goal area is the dead ball line. This marks the edge of the playing area. In front of each tryline is an area called the '22', which stretches 22 metres (72 feet) from the tryline.

The goalposts sit at each end of the pitch in the middle of the tryline. They have two upright poles and a crossbar that sits 3 metres (10 feet) off the ground.

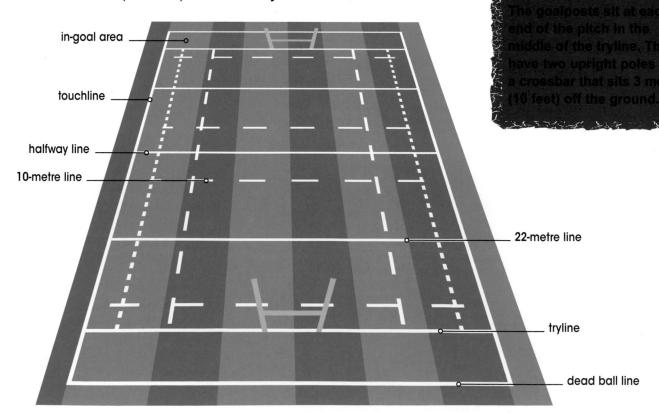

in-goal area

touchline

halfway line

10-metre line

22-metre line

tryline

dead ball line

Players and balls

A player's kit includes a jersey, shorts, socks and boots. Players can also wear a certain amount of protective padding including headgear, shin guards, mouth guards and shoulder pads. Referees need to check these to make sure that they all follow the laws. Rugby balls vary in size, depending on the players' age. For senior matches, balls should measure between 28–30 centimetres (11–12 inches) from end to end and between 58–62 centimetres (23–24 inches) around the middle.

Wearing shorts, a jersey, socks and boots, this player is ready for a rugby match.

Safe studs

All equipment needs to conform to IRB laws. Referees will check that the studs on players' boots have no sharp edges.

Protective equipment

Shoulder pads protect players from injuring their shoulders when tackling an opponent.

Headgear protects players from head injuries and a mouthguard prevents damage to their teeth.

Scoring

The aim of a rugby game is for a team to score more points than its opponents. Points are scored by kicking penalties and drop goals and by scoring and converting tries.

Touching down

A try is scored is when a player touches the ball down inside an opponent's in-goal area. Because the tryline is considered part of the in-goal area, a player can put the ball down anywhere on the line to score a try. If the ball is rolling in the in-goal area, a player only has to put downward pressure on the ball to score. Referees can award a penalty try to an attacking side if they believe that the defenders have illegally stopped a certain try or have repeatedly broken a law when close to their own tryline. Scoring a try and a penalty try are both worth five points.

Despite being tackled, Perpignan's Jerome Porical has crossed the tryline. If he grounds the ball and does not drop it he will score a try, which his team can convert.

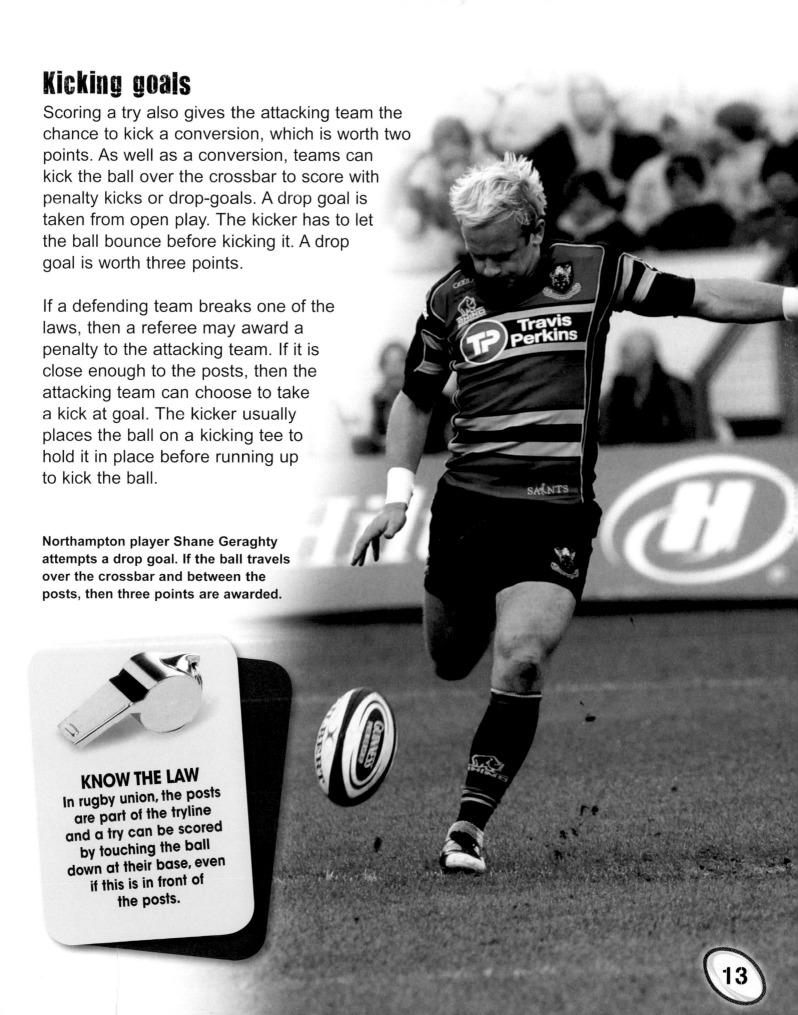

Kicking goals

Scoring a try also gives the attacking team the chance to kick a conversion, which is worth two points. As well as a conversion, teams can kick the ball over the crossbar to score with penalty kicks or drop-goals. A drop goal is taken from open play. The kicker has to let the ball bounce before kicking it. A drop goal is worth three points.

If a defending team breaks one of the laws, then a referee may award a penalty to the attacking team. If it is close enough to the posts, then the attacking team can choose to take a kick at goal. The kicker usually places the ball on a kicking tee to hold it in place before running up to kick the ball.

Northampton player Shane Geraghty attempts a drop goal. If the ball travels over the crossbar and between the posts, then three points are awarded.

KNOW THE LAW
In rugby union, the posts are part of the tryline and a try can be scored by touching the ball down at their base, even if this is in front of the posts.

13

Stopping and starting

As well as controlling the game and the players, referees keep an eye on the time, controlling the match clock and making sure that the game lasts for the required time.

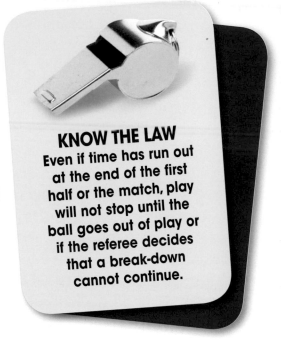

Watching the clock

A senior rugby match lasts for 80 minutes and is divided into two halves. Games for younger players last for less time and sevens matches last for just 14 or 20 minutes in total. At half time, the teams swap ends of the pitch and play the second half in the opposite direction to the first half. If there is a major stoppage during a game, for example if a player is injured, then the referee will stop the match clock. The referee will start the clock again only when the players are ready.

While the medical team attends to an injured player, the match clock is stopped. As soon as the player is back on his feet or substituted, the clock will be started again and the match will continue.

Restarts

Each half of a rugby match is started with a drop kick from the middle of the halfway line. The ball must cross the 10-metre line before any player can touch it. If it does not, the receiving team can play the ball. If the ball goes straight into touch from a restart, the opposition can choose between a scrum, lineout or taking the kick again. If an attacking team kicks the ball over the dead ball line, or if a player touches down the ball in his own in-goal area, the match is restarted by the defending team with a drop kick from the 22-metre line or a scrum in the middle of the halfway line. If a defending player was last to touch the ball before it crossed the tryline, the match is restarted with a scrum to the attacking side 5 metres (16 feet) from the tryline.

At the restart, attacking players line up behind the kicker. The defending players form up beyond their own 10-metre line.

In or out?

The playing area includes the space between the touchlines and the trylines and the in-goal areas. When the ball crosses a touchline or if a player steps over or onto one of these lines with the ball, play is stopped.

On is out

The touch judges look carefully to see if the ball goes out of play. Like the tryline, the touchlines are considered out of play. If the ball, or a player carrying the ball, touches one of the touchlines, the touch judge will raise a flag to show the referee that the ball has gone out of play. Play will then be restarted with a lineout (see pages 24–25). The throw-in is awarded against the side that touched the ball last before it went out of play.

The touch judge has raised his flag to show that a Leicester player (red and green stripes) has stepped out of play. Throughout the match, the referee will work with his touch judges to ensure the laws are upheld.

KNOW THE LAW
If a ball is flying out into touch, a defending player can jump backwards and knock the ball back into play without giving away a lineout, providing his feet do not touch the ground.

Special laws

There are a few laws involving the touchlines that players should know. For example, a player without the ball who has one foot in touch is out of play. As a result, if he catches a kick or picks up a rolling ball with one foot in touch, he is not considered to have caught the ball in touch. His team will be awarded the throw-in at the lineout.

When kicking the ball out of play, players need to check where they are on the pitch. If they are inside their own 22 area, then they can kick the ball directly over a touchline. If they are outside their own 22 (or if they carry the ball back into their own 22), they have to make sure that the kicked ball bounces before it crosses the touchline. If it crosses the line without bouncing, then the opposition will be awarded a lineout opposite to where the kick was made.

As this player prepares to catch a high ball, he has one foot in touch. This means that his team will be awarded the throw-in at the lineout.

The tackle

Tackling sees physical contact between players as defenders try to stop an attack. The laws of the game ensure that tackles are as safe as possible and that they do not stop the flow of play.

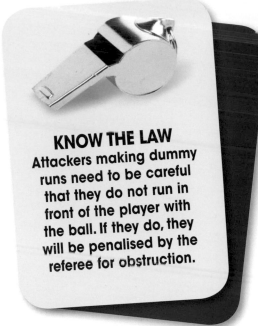

Keep it low

A player is tackled if he is brought to the ground by one or more players. If the ball carrier is not held, then the tackle has not been made. The ball carrier can then get to his feet and carry on with his attack. However, if he is held, then the tackle is successful and he must release the ball. Safe, legal tackling involves tackling the ball carrier below the shoulders. If a tackle is made above the shoulders, the referee will stop the game for a high tackle, and a penalty will be awarded to the opposition. Attackers can confuse defenders by making dummy runs without the ball. Defenders need to make sure that they tackle only those attackers who have the ball. Tackling a player without the ball will also result in the referee awarding a penalty.

The player in blue has made a legal tackle on the player in black and white.

Dangerous tackles

The player in blue has grabbed his opponent around the neck in an illegal high tackle.

A spear tackle is extremely dangerous and can lead to the tackled player being seriously injured.

Dangerous tackles

As well high tackles, there are other types of tackle that are considered dangerous. These include the spear tackle. This sees the tackled player lifted off his feet, turned upside-down and then slammed back down into the ground. A defending player cannot tackle an attacker who has jumped up to catch a kick. Instead, the tackler must wait until the attacker has landed on the ground before making a tackle.

In all of these cases, if one of the tackling laws has been broken, then the referee will stop the game and award a penalty to the opposition. In serious cases, the offending player may be shown a yellow card, and in very serious cases, he may be sent off the pitch (see pages 28–29).

Defenders are not allowed to make a tackle while a player is in the air catching the ball.

Rucks and mauls

The period of play after a tackle is called the 'break-down'. The attacking team will try to pass the ball away from the break-down, while the defending team will try to steal possession or slow down the attack.

Rucks

A ruck forms when the tackled player is brought to the ground and a third player joins the tackle. In a ruck, the tackler has to release the tackled player and roll away. The tackled player also has to release the ball and roll away. He can, however, place or roll the ball back to his own team-mates. At the same time, both teams will compete for possession by pushing opposition players away. No one in the ruck is allowed to touch the ball with his hands until it is taken out of the back of the ruck. Once in the ruck, players must stay on their feet. Falling to the ground will see a penalty awarded to the opposition.

Players from Italy (blue) and Ireland (green) compete for possession in a ruck. Players joining the ruck must join the ruck from behind and not from the side.

A maul has formed around the ball carrier. Players aim to drive the maul forwards to gain possession. If a maul stops moving forwards, then the referee will shout 'use it or lose it'. Attacking teams have to remove the ball from the maul to continue play. If they do not, the referee will award a scrum to the defending side.

Mauls

If a tackled player stays on his feet and a third player joins the tackle, then a maul forms. Attacking team-mates will form up behind and on either side of the ball carrier to secure possession. They aim to push the defenders back and move the ball back through the maul to their team-mates. At the same time, defenders will try to steal possession or slow down how quickly the attackers can get the ball out of the maul. This can give other defenders more time to organise a defence. As with a ruck, players can join the maul only from directly behind it.

Scrums

After a minor infringement occurs, a scrum is used to restart play. Minor infringements include knock-ons, if play has ground to a halt, or if a dangerous situation has occurred.

Awarding a scrum

A knock-on is when a player drops the ball and it rolls or bounces forwards. While backwards or sideways passes are allowed, passing the ball forwards is illegal. If the ball is knocked-on or passed forwards, the referee will stop play and award a scrum to the opposition. Also, if too many players have fallen to the ground in a ruck, the referee may decide that the situation is dangerous. He will stop play and award a scrum to the side that was last moving forwards.

BALL IN HAND

The props, hooker and second row forwards are sometimes referred to as the 'tight five' because of their role in the scrum.

Ireland's Geordan Murphy drops the ball forwards after a tackle. The referee will award a scrum to the Italian team.

The South Africa and England forwards form up for a scrum. Scrums are a potentially dangerous situation as 16 players are about to crash into each other. Scrummaging laws are designed to slow down how quickly the players come together to reduce any danger.

Setting the scrum

Scrums involve the forwards. These are the players wearing numbers one to eight. Both sets of forwards form up facing each other, with the referee between them. The referee will shout 'crouch… touch… pause… engage'. The two sets of forwards are not allowed to engage with each other until the final instruction.

After the scrum has formed, all the players must stay on their feet. The attacking scrum-half must feed the ball down the middle of the tunnel between the two sets of players for his hooker to strike back. The hooker is not allowed to lift his feet early. If any scrummaging law is broken, the referee will award a free-kick or a penalty to the opposition (see pages 26–27), depending on the offence.

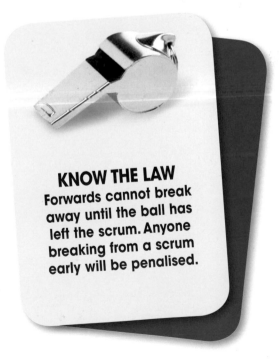

KNOW THE LAW
Forwards cannot break away until the ball has left the scrum. Anyone breaking from a scrum early will be penalised.

Lineouts

When the ball goes out of play along one of the touchlines, the referee will award a lineout to restart the match.

Forming the lineout

The team awarded the throw-in decides how many players stand in the lineout – there must be at least two players from each team. The opposition cannot have any more players in the lineout than the attacking side. While the player throwing in the ball stands opposite the spot marked by the touch judge, his team-mates and the opposition players form two lines in front of him. They must stand between the two dashed lines that run parallel to the touchline. Lineout players cannot move outside of these lines or close the gap between the opposition until the ball has crossed the first of the dashed lines.

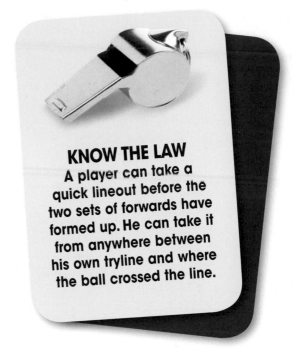

KNOW THE LAW
A player can take a quick lineout before the two sets of forwards have formed up. He can take it from anywhere between his own tryline and where the ball crossed the line.

When the two teams line up for a lineout, they must stand 1 metre (3.3 feet) apart.

Lineouts in action

The player throwing in the ball has to make sure that it is thrown down the middle of the lineout. If the throw is not straight, the referee will give the opposition the option of having a scrum or taking the lineout again themselves. In matches for younger age groups, players must jump on their own. At senior levels, however, players can be lifted by their team-mates. Opposition players cannot pull or grab a jumping player and they cannot tackle the jumper while he is being lifted into the air. Such an action would be dangerous play and a referee would award a penalty.

The South African forwards lift Victor Matfield in the air to catch the lineout throw.

Italy's Sergio Parisse has grabbed Paul O'Connell of Ireland in a lineout. This is dangerous play and will result in a penalty awarded to Ireland.

Penalties and free-kicks

A referee will award a penalty or free-kick when certain fouls have occurred or laws have been broken.

Taking a penalty

When a team is awarded a penalty, players can choose to kick the ball out of play. If so, they will be awarded a lineout where the ball crossed the touchline. They can also choose to take a quick penalty. Here, an attacker taps the ball with his feet before running or passing it. If the penalty is awarded near to the posts, the attacking team can kick at goal to score three points (see pages 12–13). Alternatively, they can choose to take a scrum. If they are close to the opposition tryline, they can push the opposition back to score a pushover try.

Taking a free-kick

Teams awarded a free-kick also have a number of options. They can choose to kick the ball out of play, but, in this case, the opposition will be awarded the lineout. As with a penalty, they can also choose to take a quick free-kick. A team that has been awarded a free-kick, however, cannot choose to take a kick at goal, and they are not allowed to attempt a drop goal until an opposition player has touched the ball.

When a player takes a penalty kick at goal, he can rest the ball on the kicking tee to make it easier to kick.

This referee is indicating a free-kick. He raises his arm, bending it square at the elbow. His arm will be pointing towards the team that has been given the free-kick.

KNOW THE LAW
Opposition players must retreat at least 10 metres (33 feet) away from a free-kick or a penalty. They are not allowed to move until the kick has been taken.

Red and yellow cards

As well as awarding penalties and free-kicks, referees can also use yellow and red cards to punish players who commit serious offences or who repeatedly break one of the laws.

Yellow card

Serious offences, such as a dangerous tackle or violent conduct, will see the referee show the offending player a yellow card. This means that the player is sent to the 'sin bin'. He must leave the pitch for ten minutes and his team has to continue with one less player for that time. Once the ten minutes are over, the player can return to the pitch and carry on playing.

The referee has shown a yellow card to Montpellier's Lubbe Rickus after he has caused a serious infringement. He has to leave the pitch for ten minutes.

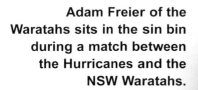

Adam Freier of the Waratahs sits in the sin bin during a match between the Hurricanes and the NSW Waratahs.

Red card

If a player commits a very serious offence, such as kicking or punching another player, the referee can show him a red card. The player has to leave the pitch immediately and his team must continue with one less player.

Players can also be punished after a game has finished. Match officials will study a video of a game to see if there has been any violent conduct that the referee has missed. They can then summon a player to sit before a panel. If found guilty, the player could be banned for a number of matches. This procedure is known as citing.

> *To me, that is never part of the game, I could never condone actions like that.*
>
> British and Irish Lions coach
> **Ian McGeechan**
> on eye gouging

What it takes to be...

A top referee

Jonathan Kaplan

The most experienced Test referee of all time, Kaplan has broken a number of records. These include refereeing the most Tests involving the same team (New Zealand), the most Bledisloe Cup matches, the most Tri Nations matches and the most Six Nations matches.

Career path

- 1991 Makes first-class debut.

- 1993 Appointed to South Africa's national panel of referees.

- 1996 Referees his first Test.

- 1999 Becomes first referee to take charge of 50 Tests.

- 1999 Appointed a touch judge for the Rugby World Cup.

- 2003 Referees quarter final of Rugby World Cup.

- 2007 Takes charge of Rugby World Cup semi-final between England and France.

- 2009 Referees Super 14 final.

Jonathan Kaplan is the only referee to have taken part on four tours involving the British and Irish Lions.

Glossary

Bledisloe Cup games contested between Australia and New Zealand.

dead ball line the line that marks either end of the pitch.

break-down the period immediately after a tackle has been made.

dummy a technique where a player pretends to perform a move to trick a defender.

first class a country's top level rugby.

infringement when one of the laws of the game has been broken.

maul a formation of players brought around the ball carrier, who is still in possession of the ball and has not been brought to the ground.

open play play not from a set-piece.

possession when a team has the ball.

ruck a loose formation of players created around a free ball, or a player with the ball who has been tackled to the ground.

set-piece a term used to describe restart moves, such as lineouts and scrums.

Six Nations the annual tournament played between the national teams of England, Ireland, Scotland, Wales, France and Italy.

Test a game between two international rugby teams.

Tri Nations the annual tournament played between the national teams of Australia, New Zealand and South Africa.

Books

Training to Succeed: Rugby by Rita Storey (Franklin Watts, 2009)
Sporting Skills: Rugby by Clive Gifford (Wayland, 2008)
Inside Sport: Rugby by Clive Gifford (Wayland, 2007)

Websites

www.irb.com/lawregulations/index.html
The IRB covers all the current laws of the game on their website.

www.planet-rugby.com
An international website with coverage of leagues, national teams and laws.

Index

RUGBY FOCUS

Contents of all titles in the series: